The Crane Wife

The Crane Wife

Sharon Hashimoto

Co-winner of the 16th Annual
Nicholas Roerich Poetry Prize

STORY LINE PRESS
2003

Published by Story Line Press
Three Oaks Farm, PO Box 1240, Ashland, OR 97520-0055
www.storylinepress.com

This publication was made possible thanks in part
to the generous support of the Nicholas Roerich Museum,
and our individual contributors.

Cover art by Kim Spence
Author photo by Michael Spence
Cover design by Sharon McCann
Book design by Lysa McDowell

Library of Congress Cataloging-in-Publication Data
Hashimoto, Sharon.
  The crane wife / Sharon Hashimoto.
    p. cm.
  ISBN 1-58654-030-0
  1. Japanese Americans—Poetry. 2. Northwest, Pacific—
Poetry.
    I.Title.
PS3558.A72346 C73 2003
811'.54—dc21
                                        2003011250

ACKNOWLEDGMENTS

Grateful acknowledgment is given to the following periodicals where some of these poems appeared:

The American Scholar: 73, 75; *Bainbridge Island Calendar 1988:* 22; *Colorado Review:* 25; *Carolina Quarterly:* 30; *Crab Orchard Review:* 67; *Crosscurrents:* 65; *Image:* 55; *Ironwood:* 101; *Kansas Quarterly:* 70; *Many Mountains Moving:* 64; *Milkweed Chronicle:* 54, 81; *Montage:* 47; *POETRY:* 17, 20; *Poetry Northwest:* 85; *Prairie Schooner:* 37, 74, 100; *Quarry West:* 28; *the Seattle Review:* 23, 49, 66; *Shenandoah:* 44, 61; *The Written Arts:* 18, 32, 34. "On a Slow Ferry to Victoria" (36) was included in *Ferry Tales from Puget Sound.* "Eleven A.M. On My Day Off, My Sister Phones, Desperate for a Babysitter," (60) was included in *Forbidden Stitch: An Asian American Women's Anthology.*

Some of these poems are reprinted from the chapbook, *Reparations* (Brooding Heron Press, Waldron Island, 1992).

Heartfelt thanks to Allen Braden, John Davis, Susan Landgraf, Judy Lightfoot, Robert McNamara, Sati Mookherjee, Ann Spiers, and Bonnie Wallace-Hosterman for their encouragement and valuable suggestions.

For Michael,
who flies with me

TABLE OF CONTENTS

I. FROM HER EYRIE

II. STRINGS FOR A NEST

III. Flying into their Songs

The Crane Wife

I. FROM HER EYRIE

THE MIRROR OF MATSUYAMA

"Daughter, this I give you before I die. When you are lonely, take out this mirror, I will be with you always."

—from a Japanese folktale

Mother, what trick of light
brings you back—your face rising to the surface?
Is it my need that imprisons you behind
the cold glass? When you lay still,
the flowered quilt no longer warm with your body,
I didn't believe your promise.
                    Days passed,
and even the pauses between my breath
would remind me that you are not here.
But remembering your words, I held
your mirror before me.
                    Amazed,
you looked back, your fingers stretched
to meet mine. Between us, I could feel
only the glass. The brown centers of your eyes
returned my stare.
                    Mother, how do you see me?
Enclosed within your reflection, you can't answer
what I ask—how your teacup knows
the shape of my hands, the smooth rim—
the bow of my lips. With every stroke
of my brush, why do I imagine the long length
of your hair?
                    Each time we meet, we press
closer together, as if you could make me whole.

AFTER HOURS

My mother tells me how
as a child, I walked in my sleep,
staggered to the wall with my hands
searching for a light switch
or a door she couldn't see
and she asks me again

if I remember. Lost in the quiet
range of her voice, I can feel
the ends of the room where the corners
meet, defining a direction I know,
but can't seem to place.
She watches me as she must have

watched another part of herself
roaming through a dream,
and the brown iris of her eyes
is swallowed by the deepening night.
The floor lamp casts a red
glow on her hair and I look towards

the warm circles of light
where the dog lies curled beside the sofa
and my father listens to a boxing match
down the hall. Slowly,
my fingers close like the petals
of a flower after dark

with an instinct only my hands remember.
Twitching, the dog whimpers in his sleep.
Tonight, when I dream, turning
three times to the left, I will sigh.
Five miles away, my mother
will stir in the dark, awake.

DANDELION

In the dark, a square of wet touched her brow.
She tried to turn her head, but its simple weight
held her down. Why was her body heavy?
The thought pulsed, first sharp and quick,
then dull and long, a piece of string made straight.
She waited. She grew to know the room. The thin
      skin of her body
stretched and swelled. Lying still, her eyes closed
she saw her fevered breath rise to the ceiling,
felt cooler, heavier air falling
against her face, felt another body moving,
disturbing the layers, shifting them left and right.

She was on a bed. Two blankets, a thin sheet,
and an old quilt fitted her to the mattress.
Was she young or old? Had she given birth?
Was she dying? She felt a shadow lapping the
      boundaries of the bed.
A silhouette leaned close.
Strong fingers counted pulses in her wrist
like the flat ripples of a low tide going out,
the surf's foam a sea of dandelions
swaying and bending around the border
of a wide wooden porch. Each time she knelt
the stiff lace of her sleeves and collar
would scratch and poke her. Low voices drifted

through the mesh of the screen door and she listened
to their even tones blending together
the way feathery white seeds clung to the stem
and to each other
before wind blew them apart and far away.

THE NORTHEAST FIELD

He wanted to tell her about the smell
of the soil, how it clung to his hands
and his hair, how the warm earth pulled

at his feet until he bent and stumbled
in the trail of the plow. There stood
the horse, silent in a knowledge of fences

and stumps, of the metal bit held gently
in a soft fleshy mouth. But the look
that she wore was of patches, heavy threads

stitched deep into the knees of his work.
He couldn't speak of the sun rubbing against
the shirt on his back or of the northeast field

where the furrows were crossing and re-crossing.

WATCHING THE HOUSE

Alone, for a while,
in my parents' house,
I open doors
into another country,
visit rooms
where I am a stranger
to a new kind of light dulling
the walls. Something

about the tilt
of a picture
and the settling
of the house tells me
I no longer belong

among the forks and spoons
in the top drawer
beside the cool white stove
or lined with the books
collecting dust on the shelf.

Something about the way
the rocking chair leans
back and forth
chills me, when I know
I should be warm

in the presence
of my father's glasses
on top of the television
or my mother's yarn spilling
from a paper sack. An airplane

rumbles overhead,
trails a path
growing faint
like a ripple of water
flattening out. Twenty minutes

from now, my parents will glide
into Japan, their ears
deadened by the shifting

elevation. Listening to their house,
I wonder about the silence as it folds
like the afghan over hills
of sofa, thick as mists
in a foreign land.

SPRUCE STREET
    —for A.C. Arai

I.

Walking up the first flight of stairs
to the old apartment building,
leaning against the wide white rail,
did you ever stop to see
how the backyard opened out
into rows of green and brown;
or how Grandpa, bent and straddling
an aisle, became so small and dark,
his long arms reaching, then pulling?
Staring at the ground, he must have known
that the dry earth would stretch
for miles, tumble and fall
against the bright rays of the sun.
Close to the smell of the soil,
with his eyes seamed close,
he couldn't see the small birds
on the fence, watching.

II.

Halfway between the sounds
of Grandma's black shoes on the top deck floor
and Grandpa's hoe breaking the dirt,
did we understand the structure

of the stairs on which we stood,
how the steps could lead us up
or down, the planks of wood staggered
in a series, how one moment flowed
into the next, mingling with each other?

III.

When did the air become cooler?
Lighter? Twenty steps closer to the sky
with hands holding tight to the banister,
my body leaned back like a sail,
the slow breeze that stole my breath
urging me to fly, let go,
become invisible against the pale blue
of the day. Above me, white shirts
billowed out from the clothesline,
waving their arms at the swallows
who dove from the rooftops
into the beginning of an arc
which would swing them high in the air.
Wrinkled by the wind folding
and refolding her skin, arms extended
in the length of a sheet,
what did our Grandmother see,
watching the ground from her eyrie?

BUS STOP AT HANAPEPE

Everyone seated on the bench has black
sweat-shined hair. A woman in a faded dress
speaks to her boy over the open shoebox
sandwiched between them. They mount the steps

to the bus, the boy hugging the box. Inside, on a piece
of white toweling, a black kitten lies on its side,
nostrils flared, whistling each breath.
The driver shivers at the tokens' clatter.

She doesn't know if she croons, "shh, shh"
to the boy, the cat, or to the bus
bumping and hitching to another stop.
Hair strands escape their knot; the heat
from her hand bakes the boy's fingers. There's a vet
in the next small city. She thinks, "he's three years old."
She watches as his eyes
keep following the folds in the towel.

The boy studies the ellipse of the kitten's ear,
how one white whisker echoes the line of the jaw.
He wants to tell his mother, "Tama's eyes are open!"
His arm hairs stand up like fur.

ELEGY: WHAT SHE TRADED FOR DAYS
—for Same Toda, 1903-1980

I.

All these years later, I'm still asking myself
Did you know? The earth was just beginning
to open with blades of grass, forcing
their journey to the surface. Still, you were cold
in the young spring light though you clung
to my arm, and we were moving slowly.
My hard shoes crushing the gravel,
I remember all those times my mother told me
to pick up my feet. But she wasn't there.
I felt your spirit leading your body
as we stopped to look at the cherry buds
like balloons rising out of the trees.

II.

Don't wait too long to have children,
you told me. But I couldn't imagine
something growing inside, something sharing
my blood. An elbow, a hand,
the humped curve of a back—how hard
would they press to get out?

III.

When the doctor said, no salt, you couldn't eat
without guilt, without looking back.
To trade how many days for this piece of fish,
for this pickled plum, for this splash
of yellow radish on a bed of white rice?
We watched the fullness fall away from your face,
your bones reveal themselves in your hands
as your body thinned to its purest concentration.

IV.

You looked asleep,
vulnerable to a moth circling the room
but I felt no warmth trapped between your fingers
when I held them, no heart or lungs
beating, breathing. No harbor to entice you
back home.

V.

I couldn't understand how you could be strong
without food, so strong in yourself
it didn't matter that you were dying alone.
Holding fast to yourself,
was there pain when you slipped forward
from the bed to the floor? In those last moments,
did you feel yourself like salt
rubbed deep into a wound?

FOUR WEEKS UNEMPLOYED:
I FAIL THE WATER DEPARTMENT'S
LIFT AND CARRY EXAM

My cheek feels the rough touch—
burlap hugged close in my arms.
A man repeats the warning:
Lift with your legs, not your back.

Burlap hugged close in my arms,
I raise 30 pounds of soil to the table,
lifting with my legs, not my back.
The shifting sack has no bottom.

How to raise 40 pounds of soil to a table?
I balance the weight on my hip.
The shifting sack shapes a bottom
on the ledge of bone. I stumble—

unbalanced. The weight on my hip
wants to return to the earth, spill
over the ledge of bone. Stumbling,
my breath collapses like skins of small balloons

wanting to return to the earth, spilled
of their air. At 50 pounds, my body knows its limits.
My breath collapses like skins of small balloons
holding everything together. But I can't escape

beyond a body's limits.
I want a job, a secure position
to hold everything together. I can't escape
the words of my mother and father:

You need a job, they say, a secure position.
Late nights, I fell asleep listening
to the words of my mother and father.
When did they let go of their dreams?

Late nights, did they fall asleep listening
to each drop of rain breaking against the roof,
remember how the sky let go of its dreams?
I pulled the illusion of warmth close to my body,

folded myself into rain breaking against the roof.
My cheek feels the rough touch
of burlap. Two minutes to finish,
a man repeats the warning.

FROM A SECOND STORY WINDOW, I WATCH TWO GIRLS, ONE LEAVING

She grips the handle tighter
and I know how the touch of metal feels cold
in a space for two
beneath an umbrella,
the rhythm of rain breaking
against skin,
water seeping into her shoes,

and why there's only a promise
that binds them together
when the curve of her sky shivers
with wind. To myself, I say
She's gone. Still, that small part
of a friend lingers in a house
where a window defines a street.
But the small shape on the ground

doesn't know how high
in the clouds the light filters down
to touch every puddle. And I wonder
if the other girl saw
her stop, turning to wait
then wave,
as the world between them dissolved.

DAMN YOU, JOE COEN

I always hated your sideways winks,
the way you thrust your feet all the way down
into the toes of your Converse sneakers, hands shoved
deep into your letterman's jacket. Every morning,
you leaned against the door of French 102,
a toss of the head sweeping hair out of your eyes.
You mumbled "Chicky, chicky" when I squeezed by,
your dark eyes concentrating on my misbuttoned blouse.
        In the far corner
of the classroom, I pressed my algebra books
tighter against my chest. My face burned
behind the heavy frame of my glasses.
How I hated you for making me real.

A WALK ALONG THE SNOHOMISH

I watch geese flock to the river's edge, stretch
their wings like the small ripples that slip
away with the tide. They duck their heads under,
lift one leg high. Stepping into a breath-
like fog, they could lean forward into the flat
line of the sky, touch the low sun warm

on the horizon. But today, my hands know only the warmth
of my pockets, the hole where the fabric stretched
thin, the cold touch which slows and thickens. The flat
slap of a wave becomes a loud echo. I feel sand slip
through the water, a sigh pulled under,
pushed out. When I sleep, how do I remember to breathe

and exhale? How will my lungs catch the breath
escaping through my nose and my mouth? Warmed
by the small wisps of blue that grow on the under-
side of the sky, I want to look up into a stretch
of wings, count the feathers as they fall and slip
through the air onto my palm, across the flat

of my hand. Dappled light shimmers between the flat
boards of the bridge. The cold air whitens my breath
and a name I thought was forgotten slips
off my tongue, rising, then fading as it loses its warmth
to a sky too big to hold between outstretched
arms that have fallen to my sides. Under-
water reeds bend, pushed in one direction, and I think I under-

stand why the Snohomish lies so flat,
why it seeks the lowest stretches
of land. Together, the geese lift up in one breath
but I don't know if they follow the sun because it warms
them or what they must feel as the earth slips

out slow and small. What I want to remember slips
from my mind. I can't see under
the water, past a reflection of warm
lights scattered in a woman's dark hair, lying flat
on the long smooth river. She doesn't breathe
or move her arms through this dull stretch

of ripples but drifts and slips silently under.
I feel the flat lungs in my chest stretch
out warm and expand. How quiet is the sound of my breathing.

ON A SLOW FERRY TO VICTORIA

The words tasted cold that day as the wind
blew them back to us, tugged at our hair,
pushing until it seemed we stood
in one position while the shores
of Bainbridge and Whidbey Island pulled slowly
away. It could have been another
time with the lighthouse on the promontory,
standing tall and smooth like a pillar
of salt; the dolphins arching their backs,
looping the sky and water. Still, I could see
the skyline of the city, the buildings blurred
with the distance we had traveled.
Above us, a sea gull folded wide wings,
beginning the long dive under. I think
I said, Remember, but it could have been
Don't look back. You shook your head
instead of speaking, watching white beads
of our breath mingle with the bow's spray.

WINDOW LIGHT

I.

Late nights, she stares into the darkness
lying still as a snowflake pressed
between two sheets, listens
to his uneven breathing bending in,
bending out. To herself, she thinks,
somewhere there is an outgoing tide
raking the sand with white water and foam,
and she wonders if he, too, will be pulled apart.

II.

When their daughter comes to visit,
bringing sugar cookies and two
crisp children who snap
and crumble into lisping words
and feet scurrying across
the linoleum, she knows
the question her daughter will ask
in a voice too low for him to hear.

She will show her the smooth brown
bottles with the large print
that she reads to him each morning
and before bed as she spoons
medicine into his mouth.

Then the children will peek
into the bedroom and whisper, "Grandpa,
we brought you cookies."

She will set the tea kettle
to boil, put out vinyl place mats
and five china cups with matching
saucers. When the circles are fitted together,
the porcelain will chime.

III.

He mouths the words of the radio,
moves the sounds through the air
with his hands. Fingers flutter
like butterflies. He laughs
with the voice and long after
it is gone.

IV.

Apples bump oranges
in the bottom of the collapsible
cart she pulls up
the rolling hill. Wobbling wheels
click on the tarred cracks
of the sidewalks, and she thinks
of the cash register

ringing up 49 cents for a head
of lettuce, 23 cents for two bunches
of green onions, the $2.14 she paid
for the filleted pieces of cod.

Slender-stalked daffodils
line her picket fence,
their blossoms still bent
towards the earth. Tightly wrapped,
they show just an edge of yellow.

At the front door, she pushes
the cart upright,
fishes for the key
in deep pockets of her coat
stuffed with a coin purse
and a plastic rain bonnet
that snaps beneath her chin.
She turns the knob and opens
the door. From the bedroom,
his thin voice calls,
"Who's there?"

V.

She does not remember colors in her dreams,
only a shaping of edges, of curves that slide
into themselves, of a quick heat and rising.
Then she is awake, her body braced

against falling, one hand searching
the other half of the bed where he should be.

She listens for a gravelly cough
down the hall from the bathroom;
for the muffled slap of rubber slippers,
as one foot drags a little behind.

VI.

The children make her name
a chant faster
than she can move
through her kitchen,
loud with white bowls
pushed across the counter,
thumbs and fingers
snapping sugar peas,
twenty closed tight into one hand.
Smaller hands touch her with their questions,
pulling at her apron
as she pinches off the tips of the pods.
They watch as she shows them how
to find the deep thread,
pop out the green marbles.
She does not hear the bed
creak as he inches himself
toward the edge.

VII.

His back silhouetted against the window
and the streaming shafts of light, she squints
to see the birthmark high on his cheek,
but the room is too dark, or the stain has faded.

From the center of the shadow, she hears
a mutter as he taps out the bowl of his pipe.
After a long time, he speaks: "Do you remember
the tomatoes we planted at Spruce Street?"

His voice is dark loam,
freshly turned and damp,
spread and furrowed
in neat even rows.

VIII.

Sometimes she watches him sleep.
His hands folded over his stomach,
fingers linked into a buckle,
a gentle clasp, he holds himself
inside his body.

THOSE WERE COMPLETELY DIFFERENT TIMES

We grin at the 'Forties version
of one Shig Kiyohara—the ink from cursive
"Always" bleeding into his shoulders.
Page after page of old photos: women home perm
their shoulder-length hair, combing curls
back from their foreheads. Men palm smooth
any black strands.
                              It was the style
for a gal to wear pleated wool skirts, bows
on open-toed high heels. And a man posed
with his two buddies, his extended arms resting
on their shoulders. Between the breast pockets,
their Army ties disappear. They all smile. We ask ourselves:
"Are they going out to dinner? A movie?"

Beyond this picture's edge, they stroll together
down the road. A Ford with slotted grillwork
slows close to the curb. The girl, her big-buttoned
cardigan pulling to the sides, bends near
to offer directions for the lost. "Jap!"
a white woman spits over the glass. The girl's fingers
fly up to her own rouged mouth
and she takes a step back
while the men swivel on their heels. With uniformed strides,
they swarm the driver's door, six hands fisted
and beating the metal. One man stops

to pull forward the patch on his sleeve. He stabs
his finger at the five-pointed star, then yells:
"We're fighting Americans." The girl sways.
She flinches at the war in their faces.

BECAUSE YOU SHOWED ME A PIECE
OF BARBED WIRE

that had lain in the dirt road
beside a lone sign
marking all that remained of barracks,
rowed and eclipsed by the shadow
of Heart Mountain, I thought
of my mother beginning her tour of Japan. What
would she say if she saw me with a piece of her past
cupped in my hand? Would she tell me if the guard tower
rose to her left, perhaps to her right
as she stepped down from the bus,
sleepy and holding her mother's hand?
Or would some things simply remain
unspoken? On the plane, she would be napping,
the pages of a Sunset Magazine
fanned by her breath. The small shutters closed,
the movie would flash by, unremembered.
But outside, clouds would buoy up the wings,
buffet the metal. A suitcase in each hand, she'll wait
patiently while my father scowls, passing
through customs under neon signs
she won't understand. Into Tokyo, they'll continue.
I turn the knotted path of wire smelling of ghost dust,
touching the barbs that held everything in.

II. STRINGS FOR A NEST

URASHIMA TARO

"Yesterday, you saved the life of a tortoise. I
thank you for I was that tortoise. Stay with
me here in my father's undersea palace."
—from a Japanese folk tale

How quickly the sea pulls away
from my body, leaving
the puckered edge of each wave
on my skin—the crab-like claws of my hands
still clinging to the sides of her box—
only the feeble clasp of my grip
holds me together. Once the lid
was pushed ajar, I couldn't hold back
the years, the cramped muscles
of my back humping with strain.
Smooth-faced, I didn't believe
my youth was a gift, so lost was I
in the flowing scarves of her arms.
But if she knew I would forget, why
did she warn me? My head breaking
through the ceiling of her world,
returned to my own—what I saw blurred
was not what I remembered. And when
I stood ringed by broken stones
of my parents' home, the long day
stretching behind, her box appeared
beside me. Slowed now with the centuries
I thought were days, eyes chasing
my watered reflection, I listen for her call
echoing my name.

SEEING THE DUCK WITH MY
FIVE-YEAR-OLD NIECE

What we see first is the withered stem
of a neck, the green head spread
and blooming. A scent, like fear

when something comes apart,
rises between us. Stiff, a broken wing
flaps with the incoming waves.

Lake water uncovers flesh
beneath feathers and what we know
was a duck rots slowly away.

I say: Don't look.
But already, the stick in her hand
begins to probe the body.

> *Here was his heart,*
> *his lungs, his stomach*
> *half-full of small fish.*

Piece by piece, I grow older,
afraid she'll ask:
What's "dead"?

WONDER BREAD

A thin rain is blowing all around us.
The mud flaps of your bicycle wheels catch
the broken puddles and send out a spray.
It splatters my penny loafers
and there's a dark border around my skirt
where the hooded jacket doesn't reach. Gruffly,
you huff at me: Keep those feet away
from the spokes. I sit side-saddle, balanced
on the crossbar, hanging onto a sack of Wonder Bread.

Tank-like Buicks, Fords, and Chevrolets
crowd the main road; their silhouettes overlap
and deepen the dusk. Dutiful brother, you've come to collect me
from my Brownie meeting. In the window of an IGA store,
I glimpse our reflection. You, me, and a dangling
brown bag on a Schwinn streak by.

The pencil of your headlight grows stronger
as we turn down Holly, past the overgrown hedge
of a darkened house. You lean forward into the night.
Standing up, legs pumping the pedals,
your fingers curve around the hand brakes.

We are close but not touching. Wind plays
through the gaps. As I listen to your ragged breathing,
I shrink myself out of your way. The red letter "W"
widens the tear in the sack. Ahead lies the curb
where the bread will slip from my grasp.

THE BACKSEAT WAR

My pigeon-toed grandmother rode 100 miles
straddling our old Ford's transmission hump—
her left foot planted on my brother's side of the back seat,
her right foot on mine. When the rear wheels hit
a bump, we could hear her knees knock beneath the afghan
she spread over our laps. At first, she fed us
butterscotch, horehounds, and taffy pulled
from her sweater's pockets—anything to keep
our mouths busy. Furiously we sucked our sweets.

Ruffling his cowlicky hair, Grandma went on
about how big Steve had grown. When had he crawled out
of a Buddha-like baby fat into this skinny boy? Did he
remember a gold book of matches, Popeye's shrill bark,
and almost setting the house on fire? I had been
easy, a little doll in pink petticoats who seldom cried.

First to finish chewing his taffy my brother leaned forward
and pulled his sweatshirt sleeves over his hands.
"Hey Monkey Arms," he aped. "Show Grandma
your banana feet." I shot my tongue out.
Steve hooted as he watched the yellow flash
of my candy arc into Grandma's lap.
Thrashing beneath the blanket, I tried
to swing my fist at my brother's face.

Grandma grabbed my wrist and hissed, "Don't hit,"
in her broken English. Suddenly, the car felt full of words

against me. Pressing my lips together, I turned
to glare out the window, to count pigs and swaybacked
horses in their corrals. Nothing was ever fair.
Nobody rooted for me when I lost my red checkers
to Steve's double-jump. On my side of the road,
every barn we passed was tilted, its mossed-over
roof caved in the middle. Grandma slipped
an extra butterscotch between my fingers,
then patted the back of my hand. "Hard
to be good," she whispered. I laid my head
against her shoulder, snuggling closer
to the peppery smell of her cardigan sweater.

I woke to a sharp left turn—a thermos,
comic books, and Grandma's rump sliding into me.
The Ford stopped. With one hand on my knee,
my grandmother rolled down the window. Her chin
lifted up as her eyes took in a tall pine
with half dead limbs. Blackberry thickets
overwhelmed the field. Grandma said, "Before the war,
Buddhist Church stood there." I followed the length
of her outstretched arm to its worn nail. Her finger
wobbled as if she were accusing the air. Sitting stiffly,
she murmured, "Everyone brought special things
to be saved. We couldn't put the piano in suitcase."
The grin on my face died when she added: "After camp,
we came back here. Roll-top desk, our round oak table—
        all broken
or burned. Steve elbowed his way over our laps.

The cold wind tangled strands of our hair. Feebly,
I slapped at the weight of my brother's hand
pushing me aside. Frowning with his teeth,
Steve chattered: "Why did we come?
Nothing's here but a beat-up gas station."

I watched Grandma's neck grow red, the throat muscles
tighten the way she bit back onion fumes
as she peeled away the layers. "Camp"—the word
made me think of Girl Scout cookouts. There'd been
tin can lanterns drilled with nails, planks from an apple crate
hammered into a makeshift table. Once Grandma
had spoken of four people crowded into one small room
before she turned because something was in her eye.
I could see my grandmother start to snap
"sit down" at Steve. But what escaped her lips was a slow sigh
and the sour smell that comes with the aftertaste of candy.

INTERNED IN THE HEART OF THE COUNTRY, MY GRANDFATHER SEARCHES FOR FOSSILS

Watching the dust scurry away
from his feet, he must have thought
of the weight of waves
as they curled, then flattened
into a ripple and how the sun always floated
to the surface in pieces. There, in Wyoming,
pale sand could have slipped
like silk through his fingers, leaving
the fossil in the palm of his hand,
the empty print of a conch
still hard and precise
where the long grooves once fluted
the water. Turning from the mountain
to the flat yellow land, did he feel
the slow drift of tides
surround him, the horizon pressing
miles on his eyes? Perhaps
loose grains of stone crumbled at his touch
when he glimpsed the thin pole of his shadow
pointing east. What did he look for
on the long journey back
as one step followed the other?
Years later, my mother would tell me
how she'd lie awake in her narrow cot
and wait
for the small sounds of her father's return.

A SOUND LIKE RAIN

Sara watches a rubber ball
drop down, bounce up
and she snatches the metal stars
in threes from the pile. Each prong
pokes deep into the caves of her fist,
worrying their shape onto her palm.
From inside the concrete stairs,
heat rises slowly like footsteps beyond
the screen door where her mother is ironing
a tablecloth, her father's pants,
a sleeveless blouse, humming softly to herself.
Somewhere, far away, a phone rings.
Echoes vibrate in groups of three.
She listens for her mother's voice
but there is only a sound like rain.

***

Upon waking, she doesn't know what time
of the night it is. Lifting her hands
to rub her eyes, she cannot see the fingers
she uses to shape the pointed ears
and long snout of a dog, a butterfly,
the head of a swan. Shadows fainter
than half-remembered dreams cling to the wall
with no clear cut shape or border.

***

With the thick-lipped man who is Uncle Nobs
squeezed tight beside her in an overstuffed chair,
she opens the photo album, splits the book apart.
Cream colored pages fall into halves and she breathes
the dried smell of trees. Thinking of cottonwood
drifting in warm air, she fingers the picture
of a dark haired boy, arms continuing the long swing
of a baseball bat; the ball, a short grey blur.
Uncle Nobs sighs, a heavy wheezing sound,
explains, "That was your father."

***

Late afternoon, rain slants in
through the open window, stains
the carpet a darker brown, pushes
the curtains like sheets
her mother shakes out, floating
over the double bed, edges
falling slower than the middle.
Bending at the waist, her mother
smooths away the map of wrinkles
but Sara remembers the low hills and valleys
of four feet pointing skyward as she stared
from the bottom of a different country.

***

The car is warm with their breath
fogging the windows and the smell
from chrysanthemums resting in her mother's
lap. Uncle Nobs' big hands
are silent on the steering wheel,
full of dips and left hand turns.
In the rear view mirror,
she spies a cow turning its head
at the car's passing and she wonders
how they can move so quickly.

***

For a long time, she sits with her eyes
closed inside the closet, cross-legged
with her hand resting on the smooth leather
of a shoe. Hearing her name called
over and over, she draws her knees up tight
against her cheek, hunches herself smaller, suddenly
afraid. The rough wool of a tweed suit scratches
her cheek and she tries to hold her breath
like a bubble in her mouth, quiet the sound
of her heart, beating loud and strong in her ears.

***

In her dream, he walks far ahead,
toward the crest of a hill,
the bend of the river, the long road
pulling him away to the straight

line of the horizon. She wants him
to wait but he never looks back
and the wind returns his words like leaves
scraping the ground, "Hurry Sara, hurry."

***

"Up she goes", Uncle Nobs grunts
as he lifts Sara to his shoulder
so she can see the squirrel's lair
in the cherry tree, high up
with the telephone poles and sunlight
tangled in a cobweb of branches.
Her eyes follow the arrow of her uncle's arm
and he asks in his too loud voice,
"Over there, do you see?"

***

She thinks of her mother
as an incomplete word she whispers
to the wall, the ceiling,
shattering the air that feels
cool and grey; of the hands,
so careful now, brushing
damp hair away from her face
like small birds gathering
string for a nest. Then she remembers
her cheek warm on a soft breast,
a circle of arms holding her close,

rocking back and forth towards sleep,
her mother's voice crooning,
"It's all right. It's all right."
as if she could have made it come true.

ELEVEN A.M. ON MY DAY OFF, MY SISTER PHONES, DESPERATE FOR A BABY-SITTER

Sitting in sunlight, the child
I sometimes pretend is my own
fingers the green weave of the rug
while the small shadow of her head falls over
a part of my lap and bent knee. At three,
she could be that younger part of myself, just beginning
to remember how the dusty warmth feels on her back.
"Are you hungry?" I ask. Together we open
the door of the refrigerator. One apple sits
in the vegetable bin but she gives it to me,
repeating her true mother's words "to share".
Turning the round fruit under the faucet,
the afternoon bright in my face, I look down
at a smile in the half moons of her eyes
and for a moment, I'm seven, looking up
at my childless aunt in Hawaii,
her hands and the long knife peeling
the mango I picked off the tree, rubbing my arms
from the stretch on the back porch
to an overhead branch. Plump
with the island's humidity, it tasted tart
like the heavy clatter of rain on a June Sunday.
"Careful," my niece warns as I slice the apple sideways
to show her the star in the middle.
She eats the core but saves the seeds
to plant in the soft earth of my yard.

A PICTURE OF MY SISTER AND ME ON THE PORCH,
SUMMER 1957

Across alternate lengths of shadow and light
my young sister crawls up the rungs of a ladder
caught on a skin of time for this moment, I am five

feet away from her hungry fingers, grasping
the rails of the porch, about to reach through
across alternate lengths of shadow and light

but I am held in one place by the sun. My sister
looks up, her face striped by the same warmth.
Caught on a skin of time for this moment, I am five

syllables she repeats into the air, a meeting
of tongue and lips to a shape that moves, then stretches
across alternate lengths of shadow and light.

I tell myself, if she comes to me I will
be happy with the touch of her hand in my hair.
Caught on a skin of time (for this moment), I am five

types of waiting as cottonwood drifts on the wind.
A butterfly bends the stem of a lily as my sister stares
across alternate lengths of shadow and light
caught on a skin of time. For this moment, I am five.

ROCK-O-PLANE

Every muscle in my body stretched tight as a rubber band,
I climbed onto the metal bench with my brother.
Caged together, we swung up. The Puyallup Fair wheeled
beneath us, and the soles of our tennis shoes rocked
just above the part in Mother's black hair. Then higher
we rose with a small shudder and bump.

Mom waved, "Take care of your sister." Bumping
me with his elbow, his ragged band-
aid scratching my arm, I heard my brother
sneer: "Look at that big beer belly. It'll bounce high
enough to knock down the ferris wheel."
From the Big Top, loud drums beat out a rock

and roll song. This cool dude beside me wanted the Rocket
to Mars. Not baby stuff, but goose bumps
like when the floor dropped out from under the Wheel
of Centrifugal Force. Only an invisible band
of gravity would prevent his falling. Our ride began. My brother
raised both of his skinny arms, fist high

over his head like in a jungle movie where the high
priest prepares to sacrifice a virgin, precious rocks
glittering in the hilt of the sacred knife. Big brother
hooted when my breath popped out like the four bumps
of my knuckles as I clenched the safety bar. Band
music, sticky wisps of cotton candy, creaking wheels—

all blended together. My stomach started to reel.
Who was this brown boy, his eyebrows and hair high-
lighted by speed? I felt the air press like a wide band
against my forehead. On the ground, Mom was a rock
in the dirt. Fences ran in strange lines. Bumped
off my seat, I screamed "Make it stop!" at my brother's

hand poised over the lever. "What's wrong?" my brother
grinned. He wasn't the one doing anything to make us wheel
forward. Our cage refused to swing free. My heart bumped
my ribs. Upside down, I stared at the sun at the highest
point in the sky—afraid we'd fly loose like rocks
from a broken rattle. I never stopped hating the band-

saw cackle of my brother, his high treason against Mom
and me. Bumping my way through a band of strangers,
I heard the wheels of the Rock-O-Plane groan on.

THE OUTER LIMITS

That Monday night at eight o'clock, my brother
clicked on the black and white TV. Dad played
with the rabbit ears. Mom pulled out her silver
crochet hook to twist and unravel one long thread.

Nothing she made came out right. Just when the Zanti
Misfits opened the spaceship's door, Mom wanted a fitting.
I held my arms out razor-back straight, not ready
to give my life. "Don't watch," she mumbled as yarn hung

from her mouth, "if you're afraid." Eyes shut
tight, I still felt the creature's high-pitched voice
creep up my skin. As the scratchy wool met
my neck, I started to sing "Three Blind Mice"

so loud, all I saw was Mickey, Jerry, and Mighty
Mouse scampering far ahead of me. But the alien,
a giant ant, had human eyes. "Naughty
girl," it teased: "I'll sneak under the door when

you sleep." My wavering blocked the set. Dad's hiss
of "Get down" drove me to the sofa. I wished
I could be a baby folded in Mom's arms. Across
the room, the screen flickered as an army jeep crashed

through a window. Mom sniffed, "It'll be over soon."
That's when I knew I'd been betrayed. Her stitching came
more quickly. In her bumpy loops of yarn, I saw a million
insects lined up to invade our home.

WINE

Five beads—
red and mottled
wait in line on the wood
porch railing for magic—raisins
from grapes.

Sunlight
slowly shrivels
each globe, each world of rain
smaller. She's five. No words explain
why fruit

withers.
All around her,
the sky glows, a smooth blue
skin, so full with unseen light. She
decides

the weight
dragging down legs
and arms, bending the stem
of her neck, is the vine's last grape
falling.

SEPTEMBER

There is something about the children blazing
a trail past her house to school, girls
with their plaid skirts bumping their knees,
short arms stretched around notebooks, lunches
in brown paper sacks, the whoosh of bicycle
tires and Mary Janes in step with slow shuffling black
hard shoes. The Gleasons' youngest child whistles a skinny
tune, puffing out the chest of a hand-me-down
sweater and she wonders how some things are the same,
how some things are new. But there is something
about their shiny heads sinking below the hill
like small suns melting into a dark horizon.
An autumn cold frosts her hair, chimes against
her bones. Her good ear echoes with the creak
of screen doors, swinging open, banging shut.
Smoke wafts through the air and she knows somewhere
bright gold leaves are crisping black in a fire.
She wants to say, Stop to the roses; Wait
to the weather, the birds, the trees.

TI LEAF LEI

Under, my aunt insists, always twist under,
a green snake coiling from her hands one leaf
at a time. I watch her wring the fibers,

her strong fingers crushing the blades. Arms stiff,
I feel the sticky salts of my body
squeezed out of my pores. Is this enough,

I ask. The thin line of her mouth steadies
her weaving. In reply, the ends shuffle and turn.
Chinese doves soar into humidity

that weights me to the ground. My fingers learn
so slowly. She picks another leaf to braid
into the moist chain; knots rising in a pattern.

Our heads leaning closer, I want to knead
the soreness from my hands. The leis grow
towards our feet like roots. Their ends unconnected,

they will hang open, heavy and new
against our necks. I ask how long should I
make this? She answers, As long as you need to.

POEM TO MICHAEL,
WRITTEN IN DECEMBER
TWO WEEKS BEFORE THE NEW YEAR

Holding hands beneath the bedcovers
in the pre-morning dark, we prayed
for a snowfall's quiet weight. We didn't speak
of the payments on our new house, Christmas,
your widowed mother, or how our lives
turn. We lay still, our faces
tilted up towards the skylight,
towards this cold and the firm slap of rain.

Two degrees cooler, the campus
might be muffled in snow.
Instead, I'm in the office by 7:59,
flipping a calendar page to today.

Stacking my mail and ungraded essays,
I imagine your fingers around the wheel
of an articulated bus. Puddles

crash into the curb, flooding
high heels and unlaced sneakers.
Coins splatter down the throat of the fare box.
You steer towards Boeing, downtown,
and the old Cleveland High School.
A navy-suited woman lurches to your side,
grumbles "why aren't we there?"

Water dribbles off the coats of my damp students,
smudging their notebooks on literature
and writing. In a loud voice, I announce:
"Thursday is your final exam." But their eyes
drift to the window as the sky suddenly spills
with snow. Mine aren't the words they hear.

SAIHEI HASHIMOTO APOLOGIZES TO HIS WIFE FOR DYING

Air accepting our small son,
I saw your hands when I held him high—
how they fisted at your sides—
and I knew you would be strong
for sacrifice, for other children
you might bear. Does it matter
that I believed I would live forever?

When the sun touched my face
the last time, I didn't think
of you—so sudden was the tide of earth
swelling around me. Red dirt
filled my lungs, I couldn't push
my way back to the light.
With only my breath rising around me,
my heart collapsed. My eyes died.

Arms wide with our last embrace,
you pressed me into our son's dim memory
and I say don't blame
the grass growing tall over my grave.
Don't let the scent of plumeria
feed your sorrow.

III. FLYING INTO THEIR SONGS

THE MOUNTAIN WHERE
OLD PEOPLE ARE ABANDONED

"I have no use for old people in my village. Anyone over sixty must be banished and left in the mountains to die."

—from a Japanese folk tale

The sun beats so hard against my head,
my neck bends and I settle my cheek
between the blades of his shoulders,
feel his muscles straining
as he carries me up
into the hills. Was it so long ago
when I carried him before me,
his growing weight between my hips,
the shrimp-like curve of his spine
pushing out the wall of my belly?
I don't remember pain when he broke
from my body but with each step
I feel him pulling further away.
His back bows beneath my weight.
How will he remember me when he won't
look into my face—as if to say,
this is not his decision.
Young, he can't believe the ripples
in the lake water are of his own face—
how when the flesh weakens, the mind
becomes strong. I can forgive him,
but I cannot hide from my death.
Like a puppet my arms and legs
wear his every movement.

CAMANO ISLAND:
BIRTHDAY POEM FOR MY BROTHER

Five years from now,
will my hair be as speckled as yours,
speckled as sunlight floating
on a bright surface that exploded
with my yells and small plunging stones
while yours skimmed and slipped over
the skin of the water?
                    Everyone but me
remembers the day Grandpa rode
piggyback, clutching Father's strong neck,
his short legs crooked like the legs
of a crab, his eyes looking past the horizon.
Knee deep and furrowing the water,
did our father look back at his trail?
And what did the sea gulls think
as they circled the air, of one man
wearing the other?
                    On a different beach
where rocks crowded out the sand, you showed me
a tiny crustacean lying still
in the shell of a snail, blurred
against a sea bottom too deep to be seen.
I remember how the sun lay heavy
on my back as we stooped beside the pool.
From behind, we could hear
the waves moving in to surround us.

OCTOBER

Inside the house, on the other side of a picture-
window, the man I know as my father
stands with hands pressed against glass, looking
out over the yard, through white arms of birch empty
of leaves. His breath clouds what was clear
and I wonder which words his lips may have framed

which memories might escape the frame
of his body. Like a stranger in a picture,
an invisible pane separates him from me, the clear
outline of each finger fixed into place. But my father
doesn't see me outside. The autumn light feels empty
of warmth. The blue sky wears a look

of going away. How far back must I look
to find what I'm missing? Why absence frames
my life? Into the sky, a chimney empties
a smoky black ribbon. Then I remember how the picture
on a bedroom wall is all that remains of his father,
how one day that began so quick and clear

changed. In sepia tones, my grandfather becomes clearly
defined—his skin and hair the color of earth. Looking
into his eyes, he could be my reflection. Fatherless,
when do we know who we are? Beyond the frame
and glass, I want him to step out of his picture
fill his son with himself the way a river empties

itself into the sea. My breath leaves an empty
sound in a hollow stem. Dandelion seeds fly clear
and free on the wind. More than a picture,
the man in the window is who he is like a looking
glass which only shows what it sees. The past frames
my life with each generation. Father,

you are what you have of your father—
what I have of you. Within a camera, the empty
shell of a man stood upside down on the exposed frames
of film. As the small circles of light cleared
the iris of one eye, did my grandfather know who to look
for as he slowly became the picture?

I picture my father's hands wiping his breath
from the window. Through an empty frame
we look for a moment, clear to each other.

ONE WOMAN REMEMBERS

Here is herself beneath the cone of light
from the low hanging lamp. She unfolds
the square piece of cloth around the photograph
then rests her water-wrinkled hands
on the smooth table. The slim oval face
of a bride reflects a camera's flash
in the brown center of wide-opened eyes.

I was eighteen, she remembers. The room
felt crowded with shadows. Standing
close behind, his strong hands laid still on the back
of her chair, almost brushing her shoulders
while the heavy wool of his suit prickled
the air, itched her nose.
                              Remarriage,
two sons, one daughter later; she asks the picture
where his thoughts flew when his foot
slipped on the edge and he fell backwards
looking up into the sky; how
red earth must have choked out
the light. With dirt seeping into his lungs,
did his fingers reach for the sun
like new petals of a flower? Slowly, she leans
into the vinyl back of the cool kitchen chair
and for a moment
                        she sits stiffly
in her good black dress, the silhouettes
of his friends rooted like a fence

around the grave, the coffin exposed
in the back of a truck. Overhead
the late sun torches the horizon

on an island five hundred miles away
but she doesn't know if the long legs
of heat-darkened children quietly edge
the churchyard, afraid their footsteps might disturb
the bodies. She tells herself, when she dies
she wants to be burned, part of her drifting
back to the near warmth of the man,
her eyes filled with a sudden fire.

GENERAL HOSPITAL,
MY GRANDMOTHER AND MRS. TAGGERT

Seconds after the high whine
of the ambulance's siren
and the credits rolling up the screen—
even before my grandmother's knuckles
politely rapped her neighbor's door,
she heard the deadbolt drawn back,
the rattle of the chain pulled taut.
Blue-tinted hair appeared in the crack,
the hazel eyes acknowledging
my grandmother's quick bow. Mrs. Taggert
exclaimed, "Can you believe what that gossip Lucy
said today?" Setting a plate of manju
wrapped in a furoshiki on the formica table,
Grandma pulled up a kitchen chair.
Every Monday through Friday, they sat—
fingers closed around mugs of coffee—
facing off.
            Monica's heart was being torn
by two brothers. Who would she choose?
"Rick—" insisted Mrs. Taggert. He was the taller,
older, darker, the first love who promised
to return from Vietnam. Grandma shook her head,
refusing to give up on marriage. Cupping her chin
in her hand, her eyes squinting smaller,
Mrs. Taggert drummed her nails: "Monica thought
he was dead. She would have waited."

"Hard work," Grandma countered in the English
words that she knew.
                    Across the street,
the crossing guard blew his whistle. As boys ran
their lunch pails against the cyclone fence,
snapdragons and foxglove bobbed their blossoms.
Mrs. Taggert grumbled, fingertips brushing her widow's
            peak.
Grandma looked past the gardening shears,
the crystal vase of lilacs
on the edge of the table. One pastry
and crumbs were left on the plate. Both women
rose. With their napkins, each dabbed
her lips clean.

OKASAN:
THE JOURNAL SHE KEEPS IN HER HEAD

Morning. I fill the kettle with water, warm from the tap.
Set it down on the second burner. Outside, blackbirds fly
into their songs. I wait for a hum, his fine high whistle.

Afternoon. Walking to the mailbox, I lean on my cane.
A light wind bends the tall grass. Behind me, footprints trail
a crooked line. I remember our son skipping stones through waves.

Evening. One by one, the petals of pikake fold back into buds
But I stand in the garden, facing north. Overhead, stars rise
bright as birds. When I look up at the full moon, our eyes meet.

TEMBLORS

1988: SEATTLE
Earth shifting, slipping,
what should be solid
runs to mud, to blood
sifting through veins
and the hollowed tunnels
inside a hill.
What a dying man knows
grows in from his touch,
heart straining, his fingers
spread toward the light.
But when a weight overwhelms
a man, flowing around him,
what can he cling to? Nose
and mouth—black silt fills each cave.

1923: PAHOA
Grandfather, when the warmed dirt surged
over your skin across the breadth
of your shoulders, you must have stumbled then,
standing bent by the world,
the stone raining around you. Rising again
and again, you must have felt the weight
settle into you. On your hands and knees, Grandfather,
did you curse the rich volcanic ash that muffled your cries
and smoothed the curve of your humped back?

THE FROG
—from a drawing by Selma Waldman

Picture a man's ribs
knifing the crust
of his skin, belly
bloated—how shoulders hump
to protect a naked
head. Picture him
falling, head-first,
legs splayed, flesh
flailed by the strings
of his breath, nose
and wide mouth scoured
to holes. Imagine
the arch as a spine
bends, the bony
pockets of clawed hands,
elbows and knees. See
how he draws himself
together. Arms twisting
paths against flight,
picture a heart's flare,
the beat exploding
then dulled to ripples. Think
how air slowly absorbs him,
how carefully it holds
the body's last
resistance. Think of a man's

black eyes, pupils
reflecting his fear—the passage
of light funneled
down to nothing.

WHAT I WOULD ASK
MY HUSBAND'S DEAD FATHER

You are sifted and smoothed to each corner of a small
white box, the lid snugged down and tight.
Your resting place is a closet. For now, until
the family decides. Should you be scattered
among pines and firs, or let loose to follow
the tides in Puget Sound? We've waited for over
a year.
        Perhaps, there are some things we can't
decide. What's missing is more than 98 percent water,
the spirit steamed from the body, the common sight
of your head slowly nodding as you slumped in sleep
on the living room couch. Perhaps, we can't imagine you
romanticized: a fine scarf of your ashes dusting
the mountain crags. You live in photographs
of Christmas, hands holding up the shoulders
of another flannel shirt.
        Spines compact as we age;
a body settles. Like my own shrinking parents,
you never said what you wanted done with you.
Should there be a headstone besides your mother's?
There is no Catholic God or Buddha for my own ather.
He won't honor a wake, food for the departed. He tells me:
"It's up to you. When I'm dead, I'm dead. I won't know
the difference."
        I'm not sure what I believe.
When I was eight, I heard someone say the spirits
of the dead are all around us. Such a crowded city.

As I strayed beyond our yard, I wondered about
the grandfather, lost in a landslide. What would he say
of my not answering when I was called. Was that why
the stilled and stinking dog, lying beside the road,
stared up at me with its one clear eye?

JAPAN AIRLINES FLIGHT #123

THE SEARCH PARTY
"A Ground Self-Defense official said 700
troops had been rushed to the area, but still
faced a nine-mile climb to the site, about
5,000 feet up a mountain. Darkness, steady
rain and rugged terrain hampered rescue
efforts."
—Seattle Times, August 15, 1985

They fall from the sky,
dark shapes dangling from ropes.
A different kind of rain
strikes the rutted ground. Soldiers

dart toward shapes and dangling ropes
of wire. Four survivors. 130 tons
struck the rutted ground. One soldier
scans the ribbed fuselage, ragged struts.

He wires: No other survivors. 1:30 AM pounds
his head. As he seeks a path through
scattered fuselage, ragged struts,
the soldier feels the floor wrench and tear.

Heads bowed. Did prayers seek a path through
their fingers? Men and women sit shoulder
to shoulder. The airplane metal wrenches, tears—
cockpit, mid-sections, wings, tail.

His fingers freeing the dead men and women, the soldier
pulls a trunk off a headless suit.
Cockpit, mid-sections, each wing, tail
reports the same. Children sprawl

in acute angles on battered trunks. Heads mute,
their arms thrown out before them. Other troops
report dying flames. The soldier crawls
toward the opened exit,

his arms thrown out before him.
He doesn't know man-made from human.
He imagines he hears voices near the exit.
What can sort this out?

A man, he only knows the human
task to recover bodies. In Fujioka,
there are relatives to sort this out—
lines filing past white-draped coffins.

TV reports on the four recovering bodies in Fujioka—
a stewardess, two girls, a mother.
Relatives line past the white-draped coffins.
Daylight sharpens a hill's long gash.

The stewardess, the two girls, the mother
all fell from the sky. The soldier looks up.
Daylight sharpens a hill's long ash,
the different types of rain.

OBON: FESTIVAL OF THE DEAD
"Families and many children were said to be
aboard, returning to observe the national Obon
Festival."
　　—compiled from news services

For days, we've whipped the floor mats
with bamboo switches. Hot padded cloths
polished porch floors. We've dusted the bronze Buddha,
wiped off the tablet etched with ancestor names,
arranged incense and sacred books.
O Shorai Sama, we murmur and remember the spirit
of all our lost children, mothers and fathers.

Before sunset, we leave our home
walking by twos down to the gate. Stooping,
we bow our heads. One pair of hands strikes
with flint and steel the fire of purity. Thirteen
hemp stems, a small heap of grass, blaze.
Except for these fires, the town is silent, dusty.

The temple swings open its doors,
pushing the shoji back. White lanterns glow.
We remind the young of O Shorai Sama,
who rides his snow-colored steed
forward from the shores of the unknown.
For him, everything must be simple and clean.

We rise and walk on the edges of the path,
two by two, but wide apart, leaving the sacred space
between us. When we reach the temple, we strike
the gong for our guests. We can almost hear
galloping in the August wind.

PAGES FROM A POCKET CALENDAR
"After the initial panic, passengers followed
the crews' instructions to put on life vests.
Everyone was sitting with a belt tightened.
They were calmly wearing them, looking at
safety pamphlets."
　　　　　—Yumi Ochiai, stewardess, survivor

Days and appointments
fly through my fingers. I search
for an empty page.

Each jolt rocks my pen.
Curved letters fight with straight lines.
Who can read my thoughts?

I write: Tsuyoshi,
help your mother. Work hard. I
want you to be strong.

Beside me, a man
scrawls names. He shoves his wallet
in the airsick bag.

IN THE SHADOW OF THE STARS

"Japanese singer, Kyu Sakamoto, whose song
'Sukiyaki' was an international hit in 1963, was a
passenger on JAL Flight 123."
                        —Seattle Times, August 12, 1985

When the stewardess brings the Bloody Mary
to your first class seat, shyly asking
for your autograph, you nod, slip
the square napkin out and sign
with your fountain pen. She smiles,
hiding her teeth behind her hand,
then bobs back to the galley. You hear
her hushed squeal to her friends
like a note halfway between a whistle
and a sigh. You know the movie gossip.
You put on ear phones for radio news.

Instead, you hear yourself singing.
You listen to the bouncy melody,
sad lyrics: "I look up when I walk
so the tears won't fall..." How young
you sound, but you can't help
tapping your fingers. You're a long way
from the Paradise Kings, the scout from Toshiba Records.
You think of that first album cover.
The black suit. White shirt, open-collared.
The ragged short hair tickling your neck.
You sat cross-legged, fingers playing with a cigarette
on a box labeled "dynamite."

To yourself, you hum "happiness lies
above the sky." Sipping your drink,
you settle back for the rest of the flight.

WHAT HAPPENED
"Without a vertical stabilizer, you can't
control an aircraft. The part was found on the
flight path which veered far to the north and
west."

—JAL Spokesman, Masaru Watanabe

I. What was heard
A man in the seaside park
glimpses the flash of an airplane
wing its silver seam up and through
layers of white-flocked clouds.
For a moment, the sky seems
to swallow thunder. One hundred miles away
Mount Ogura crowds the horizon.

II. What was studied
Thirteen minutes after take-off
Pilot Masami Takahama reports:
"R5 door broken,
making emergency descent
due to cabin pressure drop." At 6:46 pm,
he yells "unreliable control" to the tower.

III. What was discovered
Shading his eyes with a hand,
the crewman scans the waters
off Sagami Bay. Sunlight can trick
what he sees. Something metal
glints, turning in the tide.

With pulleys, the tanker raises
the wreckage. Each crank
reveals a steel strut
breaching the surface like a fin.

DR. OTA, IDENTIFICATION PROCESS, FUJIOKA MORGUE

"For foreigners, the body and soul are two things. But for Japanese Buddhists, the body is the soul. So the rescuers cannot leave even one finger there."
>
> —Eiichiro Sekigawa, Japan Aviation
> Consultant

The passenger lists provides names:
Yoshizaki, Ono, Kawaguchi. Some families
gave us fingerprints and x-rays. So we learned
of a root canal in a 52 year-old man.
With the heads, sometimes we were lucky.

I used to believe the most sensual part
of a woman was the back of her neck—
how a fall of hair, swept to the side,

rode down her shoulder. She must have turned
for a quick look.
                    There is so much
dried brown blood and bone, white knots
buried in flesh. To identify even twenty
more bodies? At least the children are small.

KEIKO KAWAKAMI, SURVIVOR, AGE 12
THIRTEEN YEARS LATER
"JAL Flight 123, en route from Tokyo's Haneda
Airport to Osaka, carried 509 passengers,
including 12 infants and a crew of 15."
　　　　　　—Seattle Times, August 12, 1985

Into the stream, I push
the lighted boats away from me,
careful of the wax and flames. Black ink
on rice paper, kanji for the names
of father, sister. Each brush stroke
comes alive
　　　　　　and we are together
in the jetliner making our pilgrimage
home. The aisles are full of mothers
planning meals for Obon. A fat-faced boy
behind Yukari kicks her seat
as her crayon outlines the chimney smoke
of a train. My father lectures me again:
"Bow deeply from the waist after we hang
lanterns for the souls of our ancestors."
Yukari looks up. She knows
my deepest secret: I'm afraid of ghosts.
To my father, I whine "I know,"
then close my eyes to listen
to the wheels leave the runway.

Sometimes in my sleep, they come back.
My body remembers the steep angle of descent
and I wake, bare moments before impact.
I strain to rise. With hands too cold to feel, I try
to cover my ears against Yukari's thin cries.
In the wash of night, still strapped
to my airplane seat, I twist my neck to the right
and look over my shoulder. I see only
the familiar line of eyebrows dipping
towards the bridge of a man's nose. In that tiny
tuck, the weight of his words gathered.
The last thing I saw was my father mouth "hang on"
like a sigh pushed out of him
into the night.

          Morning, black shapes
slithered down ropes from the sky. I muttered my name,
"Keiko," to the soldiers in their heavy boots.
They pulled away torn baggage, other seats
and airplane paneling. All around me, the sun glinted
on chunks of metal, wreckage scattered
over the wooded ravines.

Two weeks later, helicopters circled Mount Ogura.
Four passes. Relatives threw flowers
chocolates and letters from the cockpit window.
Someone poured a stream of whiskey. But the land
had forgotten the crash. How the wind clawed
at my bouquet, scattered the petals. I wanted
to bow deeply, but I could only nod my head.

Midnights, my father untangled our legs
and arms as Yukari and I clung to each other, then
        straightened
the blankets. I remember the shine
and smell, father's pomade, black hair slicked back.

This August night grows cold. A long way stretches
between me and the distant lights. Pine trees,
human voices. We are all shadows.
Clouds of gnats rise up
against the moonlight. I brush
their winged bodies from my mouth and eyes.

REPARATIONS:
MY MOTHER AND HEART MOUNTAIN

Unrelenting, the sun breaks down the white paint,
and the slight incline of the barracks' tin roofs

buckles or cracks with the four years
they have weathered. Dust and sweat shine like a cap

of heat on the top of my mother's black head. Grit
chafes her toes; her shoes scratch the rough floor.

So I imagine her at thirteen. Her memory blurs
the exact picture with the few facts she can recall,

and I ask her, What do you remember?
She tells me: Your grandmother made us think

it was an adventure to hang blankets at night
and make our own rooms, to fall asleep listening

to the wind and each other's coughing
as floodlights filled the slits in the walls.

THE CRANE WIFE

"This is very beautiful material. I will pay
you two or even three thousand ryo for it. Can
you bring me another bolt?"
—from a Japanese folk tale

I tell myself, there is no pain
if I pluck each feather quickly,
just the sudden release
of the shaft from my skin.
My flesh, raw with all these little deaths—
why should this be harder
than when I pulled at the snare,
my wings straining to their fullest
extension? Why do I shudder
with every bump and bang of the loom?
The white cloth lengthens like the snow
I scattered around me, and I remember
how each flake let go of the air.
Was it his voice that spoke
to me or his outstretched arms,
his open palms repeating the curve
of my throat? The rope gone, I didn't know
I was free. I couldn't stop myself
from following the chain of his footprints
to the thatched roof of his house.
But given back a life, who wouldn't change?
Disguised as a woman, I forget
what I want as a crane. Tonight,
when his body moves against mine, I'll wake
to listen for the wind in his breathing.